Spring Poems
Along the Rio Grande

GW00578328

ALSO BY JIMMY SANTIAGO BACA

Black Mesa Poems

C-Train & Thirteen Mexicans

Healing Earthquakes

Immigrants in Our Own Land & Selected Early Poems

Martín & Meditations on the South Valley
Introduction by Denise Levertov

Winter Poems Along the Rio Grande

Jimmy Santiago Baca

Spring Poems
Along the Rio Grande

A New Directions Book

AUTHOR'S ACKNOWLEDGMENTS: My gratitude goes out to Stacy, Esai, Tones and Gabe for their unwavering love, as well as to my friend Arturo Sandoval. I also wish to thank Brian Miller and Gene Thaw for the support they gave me, allowing me complete this book at Wind River Ranch.

Book design by Sylvia Frezzolini Severance
Manufactured in the United States of America.
New Directions Books are printed on acid-free paper.
First published as New Directions Paperbook 1060 in 2007
Published simultaneously in Canada by Penguin Books Canada Limited.

Library of Congress Cataloging-in-Publication Data

Baca, Jimmy Santiago, 1952–
  Spring poems along the Rio Grande / Jimmy Santiago Baca.
    p. cm.
  "First published as New Directions paperbook 1060 in 2007"—T.p. verso.
  Includes index.
  ISBN-13: 978-0-8112-1685-2 (alk. paper)
  ISBN-10: 0-8112-1685-3 (alk. paper)
  1. Rio Grande Valley—Poetry. 2. Rio Grande—Poetry. 3. Spring—Poetry.
  4. Nature—Poetry. I. Title.
PS3552.A254S67 2007
811'.54—dc22
                                                                2006101678

New Directions Books are published for James Laughlin
by New Directions Publishing Corporation,
80 Eighth Avenue, New York 10011

for all those struggling to protect
the Rio Grande

———————————

Contents

Spring Poems
Along the Rio Grande

We have lived upon this land from deep beyond
histories' records, far past any living memory,
deep into the time of legend. The sky of my people
and the story of this place are one single story.
No man could think of us without thinking of
this place. We are always joined together.

—A Taos Pueblo Man

The Heart Sharpens Its Machete

This winter has been a mild one, snow

melted away by noon

no heavy gusts toppled elms or cracked cottonwoods—

      they passed by

      as if I were in a train watching

      them from the window, rushing through—

everyone around me speaking a foreign language,

      traveling

         away from what is broken

           leaving landscapes of war,

           people starving,

refugees waving for us to help them,

         homes they once loved in and slept and ate in

         bombed to rubble.

.

The heart sharpens its blade,

raises a thousand machetes

in the streets, each

cutting a path through the history of lies

upheld by the law,

by priests,

by teachers,

by TV commercials, banks and loan officers.

      I tell you,

it has not been a hard winter, the cold

didn't crack the boughs, didn't split the trunks,

there was more cold, more ice and frost

between lovers than on the landscape,

>   more mistrust, more suspicion,

>   more prisoner chains drag this morning

>   than ever before—

by the river I hear the excruciating cries

of Palestinian children,

>   and I know this poem

>   can't irrigate democracy with its blood,

>   can't heal the wounded in Afghanistan or Iraq,

>   this poem's soft voice does not drown out patriotic

>   madness,

>   nor abate our lust for blood—

it whispers from this corner of the bosque

>   in New Mexico,

>   whispers for peace.

No, it was not a bad winter this year along the Rio Grande,

but beyond the bosque

>   severe freezing struck the souls of millions.

I Send Prayers Out

At 5:30 I rise to run
in the cool pools of shade and light
no flies, no gnats,
hand-sized carp glimmering lime-green
      along the river,
      I send prayers out
      to all the powers that be,
because it is Spring,
for the joy of jogging past
red berry bushes,
buoyant twigs agitated with amber sparrows
skipping thorny twig to thorny twig—
with war in my eyes,
peace in my Mechica heart,
                      I run.

To the right in the broad corn field
mowed to stubble,
two roadrunners jerk their Mohawk heads and
glare.
Geese arrive around five p.m.,
swinging from sky
         weighted bells in wing slings

                    lowering great feathers

                    spreading tawny webbed feet

                    lightly on earth.

I wait for the blue herons and sand hill cranes to return.

They have long ago scratched in me a love of them,

sunk in their talons,

nested their language in me

and birthed a migrating part to my soul.

Were they not to return,

the part that makes me human

would not be as human.

Running east,

I pray this field remains a field,

          yellow grass, stubbed flat,

          Paseo del Norte interstate on the left,

          and on the right

          a long, shallow ditch leading into the bosque.

These huge cottonwoods

have held me in their arms

in their world

when my life

farmed itself out

street corner to street corner

in menial work,

these trees waited each night for my return,
invited me in as a family member,
their branches spreading across evening sky
in tranquil union.

On the soft brown dirt other runners' footprints,
clumps of dried horse manure,
roots surface
and dive back into earth.
The path bordered with rabid brush
supple leaves,
then open clearings
where power companies have staked utility lines
like stations of the cross.

The path bends to
my favorite place
where I've sat on the bank watching the Rio Grande,
praying for the water to quench my life

with its cold logic.

I often think about
when I first
walked its banks,
I hatched from the daybreak reed shallows
a small blue heron at home.

Taking flight, the river's hands caressed
my face,
its legs and arms tangled in mine,
and it called my name—
a tossed stone
skipping the surface
until the river swallowed my name.

The river
showed me a palomino
on a hot Spring evening
lay down in the field,
roll on her back
rubbing herself, then rise and vigorously
shake dirt off

with orgasmic indulgence—
my sun-burned voice
quivers at the river's pelvic undulations
makes me burrow into its mouth
thirsting for every juiced crevice of its body.

Thank the River for Another Day

I finish my five-mile run,
linger on the bank
and thank the river for another day—

          for my health, for being alive,
          pray to the spirit of the river,
          offer its love to me
      as it carries water to the Gulf,
      down from the Gila headwaters—
      carry, I pray out loud to the water,
          my love,

River Spirit,
as I eat supper in the mountains
in a camp,
run your current into my bone canals
      lodge in me marrow-deep
      that you love me.

I need faith.

      Teach me ceremony to purify myself,
      weep betrayals out,
      wash my deceptions from me.

Walking back to my apartment,
twilight stretches out tree shadows
across a broad green field
where migrants
stack truckbeds high
at quitting time,
the baling-machine in the middle of the field,
left-over alfalfa bales spaced end to end for tomorrow.

> I give one last look behind,
> notice how cottonwoods
>> brood darker with sunset.

I place the downy breast feather I found at the river
in the plant pot with the rest—

> a fledgling hawk's breast feather,
> its name-stone heart experiencing the joy
> of learning what wings are and the magic of water.

Spring Arrives

to John & Teresa

I greet the world
> sometimes troubled,
>> other times feeling strong
> but now winter has taken its books, muddy gloves and
>> tea cups off the shelf
> slogged on, slinging its slushy coat over its icy shoulder.

Spring arrives like a busy monk,
> fluffing out honeysuckle on fences,
> blowing ashes out of the fireplace;

> I rise, shivering in first-light darkness
> dig deep to come up
> with a prayer
> enduring as the Tarahumara runner
> who tops the last hill to his village

>> at dawn.

> Let in—

Creator in the form of a river flowing to the Gulf,
let in Creator as plum petals open to the spring sun
let in Creator as I extend my hands to His abundance—
> breathe in me, fill my lungs, replenish my sight,

9

be the skin on my palms,

crooks at my elbows.

connective tissues of my bone joints,

reach to this moment

your language of flight

in the hawk soaring over treetops.

Two Plum Trees

In the morning I pass
two plum trees
one with pink petals
the other yellow,

        little signs

           that Spring is here.

    A big forest fire in Ruidoso, 10,000 acres burned
and the two fruitless plum trees
meditate their beautiful fates

        as they were meant to.

In the afternoon, I board a plane for Virginia,
second in line for take off
when a small plane crashes on the runway and we're delayed

      until the gnarled metal

      is swept off the runway tarmac.

        Hours later we take off.

A Seattle architect next to me
tells me he's building a Jeffersonian mansion

      in Santa Fe,
he describes the five thousand foot theater in detail
until we land to refuel in St. Louis.

I want to ask if he's ever created
fruitless plum trees
with pink and yellow blossoms
      that nurse orphan hearts in their spinster branches—
      each petal a masterpiece of compassion,
      unfolding its fragrant story of new beginnings each
               morning.

Arriving in D.C., picked up by Edmond and Vivek at 1:00 a.m.,
we arrive in Charlottesville, at 4:00 a.m.,
and a few hours later I'm lecturing a graduate workshop,
wondering how my fruitless plum trees are doing—
do they sense the air vibrate with my voice
when I use them as metaphors?

      I make my way to the local prison
where men are not allowed to have paper or pencil,
and I shout through the solid steel cells and bulletproof security
               Plexiglas
how plum trees celebrate the loneliness of their souls.

That evening I give a talk to hundreds in the university
             auditorium,
we have an obligation to care about prisoners,
to do something about the injustice—
and later, Vivek, Edmond and I drive back

two and a half hours to D.C.;

I stop over in Dallas / Fort Worth

and then into Albuquerque at 11:00 a.m.

and back to my apartment,

      where I greet the two plum trees,

      and inhale their kindness to the world.

The Bosque Ignores Our Religious Timetables

On Palm Sunday
nothing changes down at the river,
the wind blows thirty miles an hour,
and rain this morning
drenches everything,
urges me to
set my heart
to the river's ways;
let everyone pass me by on their way to church,
let everyone prepare for Easter,
while the river draws me into its rhythms
of stars, moons, clouds and wind,
early morning rains
pull me
where songs simmer
ripening,
to let loose on the air
and birth me anew, seed me anew, cultivate me into
a green bud
softening to a sweet yellow offering—
recreate me in the image of a river apple,
blackberry or apricot
for all who pass

to bite into me and let my juices run down their lip corners
onto their chins, shirts and blouses
in a hungry celebration of spring.

A Green Honesty in Every Leaf

The Rio Grande bosque
doesn't lie—when it's ready to show affection
it does—there is a green honesty in every leaf,
humility in each blade of grass,
brashly breaks down winter's barriers
and assaults the air like benevolent armies
warring for beauty,
          colors and scents the green land
          with odorous, benign weapons.
I join them today,
capturing armfuls of sage by the river.

ChicaIndio

Brown-eyed, black-haired

spirit violated as a boy,

I learned to violate myself as a man,

fucking to cope with loss,

reduce the ache of my fragmented self

to disassociate,

repress my insecurities—

       paralyzed by panic,

       unable to trust,

       labeling love a psychosis,

       fearing commitment,

my heart bellied up

               in an oil spill of arctic deceptions.

I betrayed myself again

       in bed with you

       at Jackson Hole, Wyoming,

           my rib cage

           a hangman's platform,

           lynched bodies

                    swayed from,

                    clacking their death spell

                    between us,

the words *I love you*

corpse worms wriggling beneath my tongue.

Sing and Dance Around You

You slept on the armrest of your chair,
a child from another world dreaming of laughing waves,
New Mexico sunshine,
of wildly insane women in a dream tribe, singing in a hypnotized
daze
shaking themselves like a flock of big yellow parrots
swaying and sweeping through the air like a song of feathers
and when you awoke from your dream
guitars and pianos wept in your eyes
searching for notes
to express your joy at being alive,
notes of music you could suddenly rise to
in that office, and with all of us holding a movie script
and reading it;
I knew you wanted to raise your legs, and kick off your shoes,
be the notes as your body gestures
become words telling us all in the small office
that life is to dance to, to enjoy,
and I looked at you awakening from your sleep
and that was when I saw yellow parrots
flutter from your waist and ankles
when I saw the guitar player in your eyes strum the strings
when I saw the piano player sit at her bench

and finger those loving chords

that swept over all of us, like a cool breeze in

      one of those Echo Park evenings when the breeze

      slightly moves the palm fronds,

      when the coffee shops close,

      when the Chinese lady pushes her basket cart of vegetables

                          toward home

      when the Low-Riders polish their chrome wheel spokes

      when the Chicano murals of tribal histories depicting

                                Mayans

               and Aztecas and Mexicans

      peel themselves off the walls and inflate themselves

      and dance in the streets,

feathered, wearing conch shell belts,

beating drums, painted up, carrying torches, in loin cloths

wrists and necklace beads,

      sing and dance around you,

      sing and dance around you,

      whose heart beats cosmically a serene

            acceptance of moving forward.

Pagan Poets

Back from Wyoming,
I go to the river,

        return
        to the chill coppery morning
        in jade silence,
        meet the new day
        like a lover's outstretched stout arms.

What I see outside is reflected in me,
what the river whispers I hear it say of me,
what the moon wishes it wishes for me,
and the breeze in the river grass merges with me,
      so the love I have
is an old river
flowing from its mountain source
        to its ocean home.

A year ago,
I didn't believe the river
and instead returned to take advice
from coffee-bar geniuses,
      Mocha foam on their lips,
      peach-cheeked muses

with napkin scribbled cures
        slouched in booths slurping quad-lattes—
hick town acquaintances
who after all their slushy solutions
eventually forget their Warhol and Kahlo theories
and marry zealots
on a mission to convert pagan poets.

Sunlight and Shadow

Running,

birds quip, fallen logs everywhere

dirt mounds on each side of the path

wide open space between the trees

rabbit brush

wild weeds and thick forest

big-trunked cottonwoods

sun shines off the leaves

larger-trunked trees, and I enter a darkened tunnel arbor—

>limbs reach out

>overhead to touch each other

>with thin black twigs

>>pleading like prisoner's hands through bars

>>skyward

>>>for light.

The path levels out

almost to the embankment of another ditch

parallel to the path,

rounding a curve in the trail, I think

how much I've buried here,

how many times I've lightened the weight

of my sorrow here

fermenting a future hope, my heart youthful again
        when I would once more make love
        in the rain, bask naked in the sunlight.

Veering off the main path
        I go left to the river,
        blocked by a big log—
to the right, open sky,
I see volcanoes on the West Mesa,
to the left big, fallen trees—
        all around me,
        other trees loom
        their branches huge as tree trunks
        stretch horizontally across air,
        each leaf a fin
in the breeze,
swim upstream toward the birthing ground light.

        Between ancient gateways of cottonwoods,
more brush, so thick
one has to find another way to the river.

        The path gets soft once more,
another turn to the right, then in the opposite direction,
roots cross the path, lots of shade,
little footpaths meander off to the river to the left.

In this spot

someone

chainsawed a log into little chunks

scattered over the path.

A black and white landscape

under tree arches

      sunlight and shadow, flash on the air.

Everything looks different

      depending upon

      the position of the sun—

         the morning is dark,

and cool, subtler shadings fade in and out

eloquently,

and when it sets to the west, each tree's trunk

stretches out with a long dark statement.

Plans

I move through my various selves,
numerous voices,
        ways of wild living,
                as I grope for a language
                to live as a free man in these times
                when words have become veils and secret codes.

River water
joins my words,
a bonding that flows
from its mother source,
to quench insatiable plotting.

Sometimes, the river tells me things
                                I don't want to hear
                how my plans are fallible, built
                        on fault line illusions.

I have a habit of dreaming,
                "I'll build a cabin here between two rivers."
And of course, this time next year,
it's still not done,
                dreams trail me, besiege me

on all sides with begging palms, gesturing in a foreign language,
   for what I have in my pocket—
   clutching my hopes in their scrawny fingers,
they scurry away through the busy crowds
   lose themselves among the thieves in alleys.

Yet every now and then, in complete surprise,
while walking down a street
   I find myself dreaming about when I might move
   into the cabin, with two running creeks,
   ahh, I say, *soon, soon.*

This Day

I feel foolish,
> like those silly robins jumping on the ditch boughs
> when I run by them.
>> Those robins do not have the grand style of the
>>> red-tailed hawk,
> no design, no dream, just robins acting stupid.

They've never smoked cigarettes, drank whiskey, consumed drugs
as I have.
>> In their mindless
>> fluttering about
>> filled with nonsense,
>>> they tell me how they
>>>> love the Great Spirit,
>> scold me not to be self-pitying,
>> to open my life
>> and make this day a bough on a tree
>> leaning over eternity, where eternity flows forward
>> and with day the river runs
>>> carrying all that falls in it.
>> Be happy Jimmy, they chirp,
>> Jimmy, be silly, make this day a tree
>> leaning over the river eternity
>> and fuss about in its branches.

Shattered Trust

Made love to any woman,

              and from that point on my love

                          was a madness.

I was what I was,

              and after a night of

              double-shot whiskies and lime tequilas,

              stumblingly

                     stupid,

back from the bar,

red-eyed and puffy-faced from boozing,

in the driveway under the stars,

        I shouted,

        grabbed my crotch,

              "My power comes from here."

My betrayals eroded my real power,

whiskey-eyed,

lethargic from liquor

              I'd fuck three times in the morning,

              grunting in

              no spirit, no love, no soul,

              thinking the whole world was crazy as me.

Reach Back to that Day

At mineral baths in northern New Mexico mountains,
when you held me under water and I heard
language rising from the interior of earth,
      to the night we watched Flamenco dancers
                          sing and clap,
their passion splintering the stage boards;
the heat of passion transforms me,
      heat of my words, actions, and breath
      transforms the room with just me
      to both of us embracing and listening to the radio
      heat transforms
      and my body generates it
      in muscles and bones
      small fires of an army in the night
      dream us together with a son,
      dream us cooking and traveling, loving and caring for
                          each other,
      heat transforms
      unleashed from my knees, hands, neck, arms
      flames flare inside me and we are together again.

A Poet's Love

Two men in me,

           in the smoke

           prowls a fearful man

           who goes by another name, has another soul

           with another mind—

           what I feel he denies,

           what I dream he undreams,

           what I hope he despairs,

           and what I love he despises—

split

every healing I experience

he infects with an addiction,

torments me with fears,

intimately loves then rejects me,

certain of my love, then disorientated,

I want it, he resists it,

suspended between commitment and promiscuity.

I need the river,

I need to run by the water,

it bends and blends me

           into the darkness of black crow feathers,

           where I listen to stones speak of our

                 inseparable spirits.

I need to be by the river
where I can dream of being
hundreds of miles away,
toting my rucksack,

> hiking sage trails,
> across rocky slopes
> in boots,
> green cap, beige pants, blue sports t-top and red
> > pullover.

My love for the river is rooted in what's fallen and what's
> transformed.

Seasons survive
beneath leaf-skin
where I cocoon my memories,
and am released a moth
in the afternoon
> to float by a honeysuckle vine strung along the river trees.

The river and I see through each other's skin,
behind the eyes into the tunnels of water-bone and rushing marrow
> into an even wider sky than ours
> a larger earth than where I run,
> a broader river than where I pray.

Ancestors Run Next to Me

                    At my side, in front of me,
my eyes are drawn to
                    a forest-shelter of dried branches
                    a homeless man made.
I jog east and pray
at the spot beneath the trees where I went out one night
and offered a fertility dance
beneath the moon, gyrated slowly, turned and curved,
my arms the branches of a female tree
        reaching to the moon with a promise
my love would last forever.
        But in my habit
        of creating dreams to break them,
        I jump like a frightened cricket through the brush.

The sun strides out to track a mountain lion,
sparrows rumor about cats,
the breeze reveals herself in leaves
and steps into the river to bathe
in rippling light;
chipmunks, lizards, black butterflies,
        hummingbirds, white butterflies, ants, field mice, carp, crabs,
            river rats, hawks, bull snakes, bees, hornets, dragonflies,
                gnats, love-pair mallards;

blue cranes on the banks of grass islands
where Canada geese stand staring at the river,
and while they are sunlit—

>what I've done and not done,
>become with time
>short, bunched curls of lime-green ferns
>that sprout beneath water
and lengthen out downstream to brown embankment hair,
carp and catfish, bottom feeders devour.

Sentries at a Gate

Two huge trees
I pass between,
       a formidable tree has fallen there long ago,
           wind-whipped bark,
               branches stripped to black stems.
     Continue on,
logs in moldering crisscross,
brush thickets and sand cedars harvest blue buds,
brim a rusting tin bucket pocked with bullet holes.

The path swerves right and left,
under massive branches,
tender leaflets suckle at the warming season—
shade a corrugated siding of roof tin, partially buried,
two by four wood frame door
crushed into the earth.

In a small meadow,
behind a collapsed tree trunk
an old washer and slop sink turned on their sides.

The path slopes, dips,
       an Indian student from the nearby college
          passes, wearing Ipod earphones.

Fresh horse dung and coyote scat on the path,

roots, breeze rattles leaves,

sunlit space between the trees,

a beautiful forest blessed by silence until

a fighter jet roars overhead the insanity of war,

as wildlife urges me to shout

out poems for peace.

Horse manure aged to green dust,

path convolutes deeper,

parallel to la madre acequia,

beside the embankment top,

level with my shoulder.

        Two people

walk ahead with unleashed dogs,

brown, shorthaired little one and an older graying-snout,

path veers hard, piercing the woods south,

turns severely left

into a different kind of vegetation, grass and small tender trees,

limber river willows wave—

I'm three quarters of the way,

roots over the path here, seven foot sage congests the border,

a bit beyond where you can amble freely,

my eyes catch white strips of winding footpaths to the river.

Petals

Today, a procession to honor San Isidro
and pray He bless
the fields with abundant crops,
children clinging to the bulky hands
of cumbersome-stepping aunts
and hefty grandmothers—human bomb shelters offering
love and security to Chicano boys and girls.

We carry baskets of petals
throw handfuls in the ditch water as we walk,
our words in each toss,

petals

rearranged,

drift away in swirling verses
touch briefly, then lines break
eddying stanzas whorl
mouth poems, ultimately
settling in a south valley farmer's furrow

to enrich the soil to cultivate corn
to become a meal
in a child's mouth.

Continue

The present

calls constantly for a reorientation

from the life outside of us—

for instance, dead tree boughs along the river have for me

been symbols of sadness,

wretchedly

clawing at sky for sustenance,

a Mexican's hands digging scorched desert dirt for water.

Regret rims my heart

so fiercely all I can do

to contain composure

is take a cue

from the nearest animal or bird—

that's what I want, to love as they love,

to know how to live

in a manner that is true:

own the wildness of my ways—

waking at midnight

the garlic sting of struggle on my tongue,

fear burning in my stomach,

I continue.

Mix My Breath in Yours

It's 6:30 a.m., time for my run,
                    I pant as I inhale and exhale and join
                              all breathing creatures.

I pray they inhale my breath, the hummingbird breathes me in,
mixes my breath in its blood,
and I pray prairie doves and crows do at sunrise
                              as I, their breath.

Beyond My Catch

Last night while driving
                 a sickle moon
followed me.
        Later, I bedded down in a sleeping bag
        in the bosque, and before sleep, considered
        the moon in the cloud-storm sky
between pines.

Pausing now and then on a boulder,
              my mind pawed it—
              my discharge paper from prison
              in the wind descending behind hills
                     beyond my catch.
Water is life.

Sandia mountains a few miles to the east
tower above the river,
patience and courage permeate stone and leaf,
          granulate granite and recouple it new,
          nozzling up from below,
                  up, past obstinate obstacles,
tunneling through and exiting the mountain.

        I pray the stone make me as consistent.

Standing on the Rio Grande bank in reed shallows,
backs exposed,
trout-fist fins flap furiously in mating rituals,

> a fat mallard sits plump in mud
>
> like an English queen
>
> indifferent to the uproar,
>
> and later,

> > a bull snake scissors down the ditch bank
> >
> > ribbons over water
> >
> > slithers up the other side
> >
> > into dead sticks and reed roots.

Four butterflies tangle on air
and the first hummingbird

> glows blue midair

as lizards and roadrunners
crackle in brittle underbrush—

> all around,

> > birds, fish, snakes, lizards
> >
> > anoint me
> >
> > with new ways to mate with the river's ways
> >
> > axe pick strikes to find faith
> >
> > trickling clear water from rock breaks.

Running

Following a wandering creek
flashing black in the sun-torched grass
and something in my soul distinctly hears
            the obscure glistening of what I observe.

Natural back-canyon springs
feed this creek
            carry in them
                        love's laughter
dazzling
between tall wild grass, delighting
the air I breathe, meandering sparkle
connects me to its shimmering thread
to something eternal.

Could I share this feeling with you,
I would say my happiness and sadness
are dew on creek-weed,
as phosphorescent droplets sizzle in my spine.

My heart becomes a twenty-four-inch trout
dripping with icy cold water,
to share with you,

then after we eat it, we climb sandstone scrolls
and make our nest
in spiral crevices.

Crossing a bridge,
over two-by-twelve planks,
                    enter the runner's reverie
                    up a slope
between flat meadows
over a ribbed cattle-guard
in pastures where hulky, dark-coated palominos huff.

The big-hearted creek cuts loose,
a wild mustang in its own bliss,
angles out, crazing a flat stretch of field
like a fishing line uncurling softly through the pasture.

                    *

                    I reach out and touch mountain sage,
air expectant with light
cries its birth in my eyes.
I startle bulls, cows and calves in the road,
awkwardly stopped, they stare
with gloomy, bulbous eyes. I inch forward
and they clumsily body-bump and butt-thump for the fence
                                        opening.

Higher, I pass a mountain lion's lair,
cross another wood-beam bridge
close to Holly's, a west coast wannabe—
rented a cabin for a year
to write her book
on backpacking bohemian hostel culture
of college graduates who travel the world
searching for their purpose, someone to love,
but after a few years, return single, like her, disillusioned
maddened by loneliness, run naked
through the snow, screaming spirits were haunting her.
Then regaining composure,
emails friends in a fit of horror
that a villager killed a calf to eat,
how this butchery should be stopped,
dismissing natives doing this
for four hundred years.

I turn off and head toward the sharp cliffs,
cross a creek without a bridge,
and finally arrive at our cabin.

Blacksmith's Hammer

Under the sun's blacksmith's hammer
I am its anvil and engage the heat
in a breathing-fire dance,
under the tumultuous hum of steady pounding
my songs and prayers blaze red each dawn,
                    simmer cool as incense, sage, and copal.

On the altar are the things I have left—
a silver rodeo buckle, the rider lassoing a lamb,
a lime-green neckerchief,
recipe book,
two stones given from a friend's collection,
heron feathers found in the bosque,
letters and green coffee cup.

Diego Rivera poster of women carrying baskets of lilies
                    I see
                    each night before falling asleep,
and I am happy, because as each day passes,
I have less and less that can hold me down.

All I Ask for these Days

Huffing along a creek, under briar branches,
up rock blast falls,
                              ascend and descend
razor thickets,
into the creek, rambling through stubble,
tempted me to pause and nap on the fern banks,
through tangled bushes,
light-headed, woozy-kneed, cliffs pinnacle on each side,
I squirm past lightning-wracked rocks,
tree clusters crowd the path, blocking out the sun
turning day to dusk,
in shadows I climb, slipping and panting
hill after hill, tree groves shouldering over boulders
at creek side,
                    and I'm thinking
                    I should go back
                    but I do not.

Memories glide beside me,
dodging and ducking wrecked weddings of tree and stone,
heel-stomp and toe-grip ledges through rock rips,
slung branches and root-butchered boulders
with black blades chipping out a passage for water,

woodpeckers knuckle-tapping pine trunks,
I follow elk and deer-grooved bank grass,
feel spirit voices speak in my direction, eyes on me,
> grip stones ravaged when mountains were leveled
> and molded into berry seeds.

Holding onto branches
walking parallel to the creek, dry in places, swampy in others,
up-mountain creek minting itself sweet and pure
to my lips, it meanders under
a cave and into glistening darkness
silver threading obsidian silence
shedding links to air, sun, forest and sky.

Rising again,
> it narrows, widening further up,
> where I decide to finally stop, sweating, sit down
> guzzle from the creek. I still have a long way to go,
> but its real—
>> I'm tired, hungry, aching
>> and that's all I ask for these days.

Ceremony

My Mexican friend, a poet, arrives from Chihuahua
and I take him to a ceremony.
People jammed shoulder to shoulder,
cauldrons brim with food, friends step in the circle
telling their story,
wounded from wars, ravaged by racism,

Oti and Victorio strum Veracruzano songs,
and we join in, clapping, praying, praising—

drink peyote tea from the ladle,   sing
drink,   sing,
drink,   sing.

A friend gives me a stained glass picture frame
made in her father's garage in Wisconsin.
She sits on the bed,
making a feather fan from hawk feathers I've gathered in the

bosque.

She has to return,
but leaves behind the feather friendship fan
and we bless each other with our silence.

I Have No Shadow

Sitting here below an eagle tree, I have no shadow;
        medicine men told me about
        eagle tree legends,
        where eagles gather during winter,
        and I start picking up white eagle feathers,
        beautiful small ones,
        long, wide ones,
        some reaching from the tip of my finger
                past my elbow—
        I'll cure them with tobacco, blue corn meal, in
                    ceremony,
        braid red and blue thread and beads at the base,
        red for earth dreams and visions,
        turquoise beads to connect them to sky,
        then give them to the sun dancers
                in return for their prayers.

I continue, my left hand full of feathers,
my right hand clutching at rocks, higher
until I come to a source of water pouring
from soft grass and lichen moss stones,
gulp water at the womb,
lather my face, arms, neck, shoulders and hair,

dip the feathers in, close my eyes and sprinkle my entire body.

    My ancestors appear

    a few feet away,

    on a fallen tree log in black skirts,

    purple lilacs in their hair,

        all around me in the forest

        wind groans in the giant evergreens.

Up further, where rocks converge in gullet heaves,
a butterfly bumps my feather clutching finger,

        I slip and start to butt-skid down

        reach my left hand out for something to hold,

        grab a cactus—

it holds,

but my palm bleeds molten hot with pain,

quills pierced to the bone,

    and I move up, eagle feathers in my right hand,

    pain in my left,

    finally reach level ground,

    I stand at the peak—

    overlooking mesas, valleys, closer to the sun

    than I've ever been, bearing gifts—

        blood in one hand, feathers in the other.

A Blue Heron Feather

A breeze comes up from arroyo willows and olive trees
their fragrance
           illuminates the air.
                    An early moon arrives through the trees,
                    steps out of the whirlpool of clouds
                    in her red bathing suit,
                    lithe legs looking so erotic,
                    prettiest yellow I've ever seen.

Next morning
Canada geese and goslings in the midstream cattails;
a huge, orange monarch butterfly nonchalantly passes me,
                         within arm's reach,
                         black butterflies rush by,
schools of ditch carp whoosh through water to dark bottoms,
spooked squirrels flurry up tree trunks,
alarmed lizards rush in flowering weeds,
leaf-weighted branches droop heavily above the ditch water,
beneath them in the shadows a Mallard teaches her chicks
to carouse on sun-glossed water
and as I jog by they all hurry behind branches—
blessed by a red tail hawk that follows above,
sparrow hawks, bevies of newborn mallard chicks

mother's giving lessons to sway their feathered rumps
and propel, float and duck heads under water.

I pass a turtle.

Then later, while running in the rambling forest
find a wounded mallard hopping on the trail,
one of her chicks terrified, comes out,
skits hysterically down the trail.

Two boys on bicycles
approach and I stop,
catch the chick
in my palm and carry it to its mother.

I've tracked the mallards since December when they came, saw

them
in the shallows mating, witnessed their clustered chicklings
fanning tails and bulbous fannies
squiggling through water, hiding in
dense cattail grass,
and I've seen the blue heron grow from a small
light-greenish-blue bird to a large gray heron
with a rainbow wingspread,
long beak, short torso.
I've watched the carp suspended in pools
of brown water,

seen them grow from pea-shooters into .45 magnums

gobbling anything in their way,

seen the hummingbirds arrive this week,

seen the ground covered with whiffs from cottonwood trees,

seen clearings in the river forest

turn white as snow with lint,

dried yellow grass seeds, brittle and spiky and sharp

stick to my socks and black horseflies

sting my calves,

black, yellow, white, blue and red butterflies

flit around me...

and I run,

sparrows and red and blue finches in the bush,

red and black ant piles mound up overnight,

bees and wasps and blue-tailed dragonflies

skimming the water

      but among all these precious gifts

      what a surprise to discover

      a blue heron feather,

      not small as they usually are, no—

         this was a fourteen inch light-blue wing feather.

            I've been hoping years to find one.

Eight Feet Below the Levee

Rows of dinosaur-size cottonwoods,
widow willows and creosote nag the bank,
tips droop into the water,
a bull bellows from a field, eager river rats scuttle in mud burrows,
Canada geese wail, circling,
    not a place to sit on this ditch,
    wild sun flowers abound—
    I surprise two mallards, seconds after two more pairs flap

                            out,

    three females and mates from shallows beneath the branches,
and a minute later two belated ones bolt off
from cattail curtains.

On the other side of the ditch,
a center of grass people can fish from,
flanked by trees crowding around it,
no room for even standing.
             Mexicans and Chicanos
              fish here for carp, no rubbish in the water.
Crows perforate cottonwoods, a horde of aroused finches
twit in scrubby trees.
I'm wearing my frayed blue baseball cap, black hood sweatshirt,
shorts, old sneakers.

The ditch road widens;

> city workers recently scraped it
> dredging up two kiddy pools discarded on the bank,
>> crows start across the open blue sky,
>> blackbirds roost
>> and brown sparrows flitter tree to tree.

Plastic gallon milk jugs float by in the water,
twenty-five-gallon redi-mix plaster buckets snag on debris,
beyond the ditch multi-million dollar gated suburbs,
next to it another electric chainlink subdivision has replaced

> wetlands,

geese move on, east to west,
settle in the very last farmer's field,
an old timber and plank bridge,
carries horse rider or truck across to the big brown farm house,
blue frame windows, tan stucco,
warped linoleum roof,
horses faces protected with cloth masks
to keep flies away, they kick at two rotweillers
nipping at their hooves.

I stop, hands on hips, breathing hard, look up
at geese aloft in formation
approaching the old farmer's field, others heading north,

> new ones from the south,

V's from the west,

mixed in with Canada geese, burgundy-headed ducks, white

necks,

lag-behinds strive to catch up.

I've reached the end of the run;

looking back with gratitude,

thankful for legs, lungs and heart,

as a gray-feathered roadrunner

on edge of the field, looks south,

thin gray legs, a black-feathered crown adorns its head,

tail flicks up and down, looks east,

snaps its head right to left, tail a conductor's baton goes up,

twitches

side to side as it struts.

A second roadrunner marches into the middle of the field,

first one jitterbugs into the access road

skirting the field, the second one hesitates

in the middle of the field,

sorting things out,

intent unclear, dashing about, racing back and forth,

quickly turning around,

rotating antennae tail testing the airwaves.

In the gated catacomb subdivision,

a lone carpenter's circular saw

                screeches at the air—

                sniveling across the field

littered with empty cases of Bud,

                    McDonald's hamburger wrappers,

                            soda pop cups,

                                  six-pack cartons.

The Last Leg

An area of scorched trunks,
lightning struck,
I've named the black monarch.
                    The path narrows,
                    storm-scrapped branch tangles,
                    some chainsawed and piled.
        Much larger tree trunks, enormous,
        twenty to fifty feet,
        create a colossal playground for birds,
then into the last leg of my run,
crows clamor caws through an expansive cottonwood meadow.

You can see a long way;
        homeless misfits built two shelters of tree sticks,
        thatched solid so the rain won't seep in,
        large enough for a group of vagrants
        to sit around a fire sharing stories of hellish descent.

A sleek-feathered woodpecker swoops to a gray elm branch,
wings edged black, red slashes underneath, pecking at the bark.

One stick shelter is round, brushwood tapers up teepee style,
the other is square, broad backend, packed dense

with wooly-weed undergrowth, snub noses
forward to a dark opening entrance.

An empty wine bottle
in the crook of a branch
mud all over the green glass.
Above the twisting path
geese and mallards nag,
the path lassos around and loops back as it nears its end,
sawed branches at the border,
wider clearance on each side.

Loping comfortably through the labyrinth,
hopping over bunches of cottonwood bark
scattered on the dirt,
sunlight crochets a shawl of shadows from looming trees,
and the path undulates markedly, up and down
toward a hollowed, fallen trunk,
last years leaves whiten the ground,
down again, up again,
ousted roots carve and splinter the path,
around silver creosote brush,
                    willows mourn,
                              down a sandier steep slope,
                    pitching up, the incline makes me gasp for breath,
                    hard to run

around trees,

left,

and I see la madre acequia,

as the path escalates,

panting,

I emerge out of the bosque,

up the embankment,

lean over

out of breath

touch the green irrigation pipe gates

that mark the end of my run south.

I Have No Answers

Sometimes standing at the beginning
   of my run, I feel tired, aching, unable
to get the joy in me to run,
but I think once I get a mile or two behind me,
once I start to sweat, and if I see
a quail, a pheasant, the red-tailed hawk
   circling above,
mallards under the bare branches
   of Russian olive trees
   leaning over the ditch banks,
this feeling will evaporate—

   I have no answers
     on this morning
       when people
       kneel reverently in church pews,
when a million hands are folding in prayers to the Lord
when people in the thousands walk to Chimayo
from all directions to the Santuario
  to kneel in the dirt, incline their heads in piety,
  in wheel chairs,
  on crutches,
  some without arms, legs, with cancer

and AIDS,

others with frigid veins of hate

others who lost their money or make too much

and it has made them lose joy,

their purpose only to track their money

    not the roadrunner's passage

    through arroyos,

    and they expect a miracle to happen

        in themselves,

celebrating Christ

    singing psalms from the Bible,

    and in the turning of pages

        ignore their hardening hearts.

        And as I jog, warm my stiff muscles

               and limber up,

I pray

to the halo luster of leaves, Christ

churning His body into leaf-mulch to feed the roots

and brush-shag for birds to nest,

    and everywhere I look, I see the resurrection

    now He is this river water

and each leaf has a certain intelligence that sings to me,

how He simmers up from Mother Earth a sweetness of

        compassion

for my aging feet, and how the path opens and each turn

I take unveils His beauty, His rising love opening in broad
spaces of sunlight
and shadows I run into and out of His resurrection,
His blessings, His love . . .

I Love My Life

       I announced
I had books to give away
      —if anyone wanted free books
      meet me outside in the parking lot
and they did, and it was so funny—
              two- and three-hundred-pound grandpas,
              skinny, graying grandmas
              abuelos flacos con barbas y brochas,
ohing and ahing over the boxes
of children's books donated to me by bookstores—
and here, because months ago I volunteered to be the librarian
at a school without books
to stock their shelves, to make sure they all had books—
              here I am at dawn
              with sixty- and seventy-year-old grandparents
              loading up armfuls of books to take back to their
                        grandchildren.
I don't know how Christmas ornaments ended up in one box
but several of the older men and women in their eighties
walk off, arms bulging with fairy tale books,
wearing Christmas wreathes around their necks and on their heads,
the women draping red bunting cloth
used for fireplace mantles

over their shoulders

like scarves kings and queens wear—

these poor people are regal, carrying armfuls of kingdoms and

dreams

for their grandchildren, to imagine they too can have and be

and break through the poverty

through reading—

I love my life,

here at 6:00 a.m., giving out books

to people who have never had them—

I am blessed!

Thank you Creator

for the fate you have given me!

The Gift Collector

In the way a surveyor lays out a map on the truck hood
and follows the ridges and valleys with his fingertip,
I too know the land of my heart.
I collect things my friends found on their walks in the bosque
and left with me—
behind the front door there is the walking stick
Efren used on his walks to the river.
On my altar is a twig picked from
the shoulder high sage brush path.
Turtle Clan medicineman Uncle Jimmy's sage sticks are there,
so is Cindy's gift to me of Our Lady of Chestehova,
and Indian poet Makadran's gift of Hanuman Ji Dave,
I pray before each morning, along with Lejia's
Virgen De Guadalupe retablo.
Other gifts from friends brim my altar—
scarves, belt buckles, teeth, sacred pouches of tobacco,
apples and chocolate, sacred salt from the Zuni,
arrowheads from the Anasazi, pottery from the Cevines,
Mechica warrior red cloth, statue of the Aztec Poet King,
gourds, feathers, incense, and much more
                    intended to assist
                    me on journey
            toward myself

the most ancient of altars
where I place only one thing,
                love.

Love is only letters
until they ignite during times of need
knock at your door wearing the face
of friends carrying pots of food because your cupboards are

                                                empty,
medicine because you are ill,
money because you can't meet your heating bill,
simple embraces to fortify you on your struggle.

Other times, at twilight, when all the loneliness of the world
becomes a meteorite fireball in the darkening sky and collides
into your chest, exploding against the fragment of hope still left,
love falls, a dirt-soiled relic picked from the ground
reminding us of a dreamtime,
a remnant from childhood when we created other worlds
populated with people we pocketed and saved in the penny jar
of the heart;
                today the heart is cracked, weathered and broken,
                a cardboard box we've carried far in our travels,
                keep foreign coins in,
                broken watches, buttons, pendants, key chains,
                and at journey's end,

afternoon overcast with impending snow,

    a gray day,

    where young women in hooded parkas walk dogs,

    lovers lay in bed and reminisce

    about their wild days doing drugs and drinking,

    when sweet music eases and soothes the dusk

    to help us bear our mistakes with a smile,

        the old box of love

        we set adrift in the river

        standing at the banks watching it vanish,

                hoping someone, perhaps

another little boy

will find it and treasure it as we have.

    But it returns,

    shimmers like a mirage of a stranger

we see coming at us from a distant field

making his way through the mist,

hungry, emaciated, bundled in rags,

waving to us as if he knows us,

    features gleaned gaunt to a basic spirituality,

    no longer craving to party, do drugs, drink, fuck all night

    but to join us for dinner across the table in our kitchen

and gnaw with wild appetite on bread,

black coffee, eggs and ham, hash browns—

        morose-eyed, scruff-faced

on fundamental groundings of truth and compassion,
cave-humility in his manners and words,
the way this hungry man wipes the plate clean
with a piece of bread, drinks the last drop of hot black
coffee,
says thank you for your kindness,
puts his cap on, shoulders into his worn jacket
and heads off down the road,

        sinking into the mist again
        as we stand at the door, watching him depart,
        knowing that is the only way to keep him.

What is Broken is What God Blesses

for Jason

The lover's footprint in the sand

the ten-year-old kid's bare feet

in the mud picking chili for rich growers,

not those seeking cultural or ethnic roots,

but those whose roots

have been exposed, hacked, dug up and burned,

and in those roots

do animals burrow for warmth;

what is broken is blessed,

not the knowledge and empty-shelled wisdom

paraphrased from textbooks,

not the mimicking nor plaques of distinction

nor the ribbons and medals

but after the privileged carriage has passed

the breeze blows traces of wheel ruts away

and on the dust will again be the people's broken

footprints.

What is broken God blesses,

not the perfectly brick-on-brick prison

but the shattered wall

that announces freedom to the world,

proclaims the irascible spirit of the human

rebelling against lies, against betrayal,
against taking what is not deserved;
      the human complaint is what God blesses,
      our impoverished dirt roads filled with cripples,
what is broken is baptized,
      the irreverent disbeliever,
      the addict's arm seamed with needle marks
         is a thread line of a blanket
      frayed and bare from keeping the man warm.
We are all broken ornaments,
         glinting in our worn-out work gloves,
         foreclosed homes, ruined marriages,
from which shimmer our lives in their deepest truths,
blood from the wound,
             broken ornaments—
when we lost our perfection and honored our imperfect sentiments,
              we were blessed.
Broken are the ghettos, barrios, trailer parks where gangs duel
              to death,
yet through the wretchedness a woman of sixty comes riding her
             rusty bicycle,
      we embrace
      we bury in our hearts,
broken ornaments, accused, hunted, finding solace and refuge
      we work, we worry, we love
      but always with compassion

reflecting our blessings—
in our brokenness
thrives life, thrives light, thrives
the essence of our strength,
each of us a warm fragment,
broken off from the greater
ornament of the unseen,
then rejoined as dust,
to all this is.

Index of Titles and *First Lines*

Contemporary American Poetry from
NEW DIRECTIONS

John Allman

Curve Away from Stillness

Lowe's Triboro

Jimmy Santiago Baca

Black Mesa Poems

Immigrants In Our Own Land & Selected Early Poems

Martín & Meditations on the South Valley

Winter Poems Along the Rio Grande

Kamau Brathwaite

Ancestors

Black + Blues

DS(2)

MiddlePassages

Anne Carson

Glass, Irony and God

Hayden Carruth

Asphalt Georgics

For You

From Snow and Rock, from Chaos

Tell Me Again How the White Heron Rises
>   and Flies Across the Nacreous River
>   at Twilight Toward the Distant Islands

Cid Corman

Livingdying

Nothing / Doing: Selected Poems

Sun Rock Man

Robert Creeley

Echoes

If I Were Writing This

Life & Death

Windows

Lawrence Ferlinghetti

A Coney Island of the Mind

A Far Rockaway of the Heart

Americus, Book I

How to Paint Sunlight

These Are My Rivers:

New & Selected Poems 1955-1993

Wild Dreams of a New Beginning

Thalia Field

Incarnate: Story Material

Point and Line

Forrest Gander

Eye Against Eye

Science & Steepleflower

Torn Awake

Allen Grossman

The Ether Dome and Other Poems New and Selected

How to Do Things With Tears

Sweet Youth: Poems by a Young Man and an
Old Man 1953-2001

Paul Hoover

The Novel

Susan Howe

The Europe of Trusts

Frame Structures: Early Poems 1974-1979

The Midnight

The Nonconformist's Memorial

Pierce-Arrow

Mary Karr

The Devil's Tour

Viper Rum

Nathaniel Mackey

Splay Anthem

Bernadette Mayer

A Bernadette Mayer Reader

Midwinter Day

Scarlet Tanager

Michael McClure

Rain Mirror

Rebel Lions

Simple Eyes

Toby Olson

Human Nature

We Are the Fire

Michael Palmer

At Passages

Codes Appearing: Poems 1979-1988

The Company of Moths

The Lion Bridge: Selected Poems 1972-1995

The Promises of Glass

Jerome Rothenberg

A Book of Witness: Spells & Gris Gris

New Selected Poems 1970-1985

A Paradise of Poets

Triptych:

Poland/1931

Khurbn

The Burning Babe

Vienna Blood

Peter Dale Scott

Coming to Jakarta

Crossing Borders

Listening to the Candle

Minding the Darkness

Gary Snyder

The Back Country
Look Out
Myths & Texts
Regarding Wave
Turtle Island

Rosmarie Waldrop

A Key Into the Language of America
Blindsight
Curves to the Apple:
The Reproduction of Profiles
Lawn of Excluded Middle
Reluctant Gravities

VISIT OUR WEBSITE

www.ndpublishing.com